M1 Finding the Punch Line

Work with a partner and fill in the grid.
Read out the beginning of the little jokes (A–M) and try to find the right punch line (1–13).

A Why do spiders like the Internet?

B What do you get when you cross an Apple computer with fast food?

C What did the big chimney say to the little chimney?

D What's red and white?

E What's the best thing to put in a fruit cake?

F Why did the orange stop rolling down the hill?

G Why did the teacher go cross-eyed?

H Why are four-legged animals such bad dancers?

I What does a whale eat for tea?

J What starts with P, ends with E and has a million letters in it?

K What do you call a donkey with carrots in his ears?

L Doctor, Doctor, I've shrunk!

M A penguin walked into a pub and asked the owner:

What did the owner reply?

1 Because she couldn't control her pupils

2 It ran out of juice.

3 What does he look like?

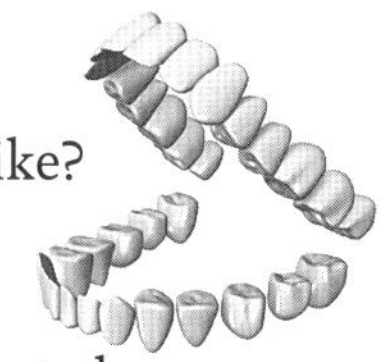

4 Your teeth

5 Well, you'll just have to be a little patient!

6 A Big Mac

7 You're too young to smoke.

8 Because of all the websites

9 The post office

10 Because they have two left feet

11 Pink

12 Fish and ships

13 Anything you like; he can't hear you.

A	B	C	D	E	F	G	H	I	J	K	L	M

M2 British Breaks

Tip

Skimming a text means to read it quickly …
- to get the main facts or ideas in it. ■

1 A first look: Look at the short texts on the next page for five seconds. Now cover the page and tell your partner what type of text it is.

It's a ____________________.

Which elements help you to find out the type of text …

- on the next page?

____

____

____

____

- in general?

____

____

____

____

2 A second look: Look at the flyer again for 30 seconds and pay special attention to these elements. Now cover the page and write down in your own words what sort of information the page offers.

British Breaks

London weekend

from £ 120

3 days

- Two nights in a double room
- Hotel in the centre of London
- Continental breakfast
- Two-day Travelcard (Underground, buses, etc.)

London Art Exhibitions

from £ 99

2 days

- One night in twin room
- 2 star hotel
- Full English breakfast
- Entrance fees to Tate Modern and National Gallery

Lake District

from £ 272

3 days

- One night at first-class hotel close to Lake Windermere
- Evening meal (for two) in award-winning restaurant
- Two nights in comfortable guesthouse in Keswick
- Spectacular Ten Lakes Tour: 2-day tour to Ullswater, Borrowdale, Buttermere
- Boat cruise (3 hours)
- Free lunch packet

Royal London

from £ 99

2 days

- One night in a double room
- 3 star hotel in the centre of London
- Continental breakfast
- Royal London sightseeing tour (hop-on-hop-off)
- Admission to Buckingham Palace
- Visit to Windsor Castle
- Tour manager

London Eye & Legoland

from £ 100

2 days

- One night in twin room, family hotel
- Continental breakfast
- Admission to London Eye
- Entrance to Legoland Windsor

Oxford and Stonehenge

from £ 99

2 days

- One night in double room, 3 star hotel
- Sightseeing tour in Oxford
- Admission to Pembroke College and Christ Church College
- Entrance to Stonehenge

English Riviera

from £ 200

5 days

- Four nights in a double room
- Full-service spa
- Five minutes to the beach
- Half board
- Tour manager
- Visits to Torquay, Brixham and Paignton can be arranged

Edinburgh

from £ 298

4 days

- Three nights in comfortable hotel near Princess Street
- Cooked breakfast inclusive
- Internet available in all rooms free of charge
- Voucher for city tour on red hop-on-hop-off buses
- Guided tour: The Royal Mile, Castle and Old Town
- Entrance fee to all attractions within the Castle
- Free souvenir guide

sunshine holidays

(01752) 27 28 29

www.sunshine-holidays.co.uk

M3 Youth Hostels in London

Tip

Scanning a text means to read it quickly …
- to find special information. ■

The website www.youngsters-in-London.co.uk gives information about accommodation in London.

Youngsters in London

Search

Home | Where to stay | What to do | How to get there

Your Youth Hostels in London

London Central

This is the newest hostel of the Youth Hostels Association of England & Wales in London. On seven floors we offer modern inexpensive accommodation. Perfect for young travellers who want to be in the heart of this lively capital.

104 Street, London, W1W 5NU ☎ 0845-3719154
@ londoncentraljh@yha.org.uk
Just five minutes' walk from Oxford Street and Underground stations
124
Ⓟ Underground car park
Open every day of the year – 24 hours
£ Adult: £ 24.50 – Under 18: £ 17.50
Need to know: This hostel is not suitable for groups

Check Availability

Hostel

Day Month Year

Nights Male Female

Check ⏩

Oxford Street

Oxford Street is where the action is. You can shop 'til you drop in Britain's most famous shopping street. The hostel is within walking distance of many theatres. If you're looking for a quiet break, don't choose this busy, lively hostel!

14 Noel Street, London, VV1F 8GJ ☎ 0845-3719133
@ oxfordst@yha.org.uk
2 minutes to Underground station
94
Ⓟ Parking available
Open every day of the year
£ Adult: £ 24.50 – Under 18: £ 18.50
Sorry, no groups

St. Pancras

YHA London St. Pancras has been redecorated and improved and now offers guests an even higher standard of accommodation. Brand new Internet café to relax in after a busy day exploring London.

79 – 81 Euston Road, London NW1 2QE ☎ 0845-3719344
@ stpancras @yha.org.uk
Short walk from Euston and Kings Cross Underground and train stations
184 – Premium rooms are available, offering TV and Internet access
Ⓟ No parking
Open from March to November
£ Adult: £ 21.95 – Under 18: £ 16.50
Families and groups welcome

Terms of use | Advertise | About | Contact | Help | Sitemap

accommodation: a place (for example a room) for someone to stay; available: can be used or found
redecorated: repaired and painted; brand new: completely new
premium: of very high quality

1 Read the website about hostels in London and find the information to complete the table below.

	London Central	Oxford Street	St. Pancras
Number of beds			
Price for youngsters			
Suitable for groups			
Suitable for families			
Distance to tube			
Parking			
Internet			
Opening times			

2 Answer these questions on the text with short answers.

a Which is the most modern hostel? ______________________

b Which hostel is closest to theatres? ______________________

c Which hostel is closest to London's most famous shops? ______________________

d Which hostel offers premium rooms? ______________________

3 Youth hostelling or camping?
Work in groups to discuss the advantages and disadvantages of youth hostels and camp sites.
Conduct a survey in your class (or school).

I prefer youth hostelling, because …	I prefer camping, because …

M4 Cooking Together

At the weekend Sandra and five of her friends (Meryl, Linda, Pat, Malcolm and Alan) would like to cook a meal together. Sandra has sent her friends an e-mail with her favourite recipes.
Now they are all online and go through her suggestions.
Here are the lists of ingredients for Sandra's recipes:

Minestrone

2 tablespoons olive oil
2 onions
1 small packet of soup noodles
2 carrots
4 celery sticks (or any other vegetable of the season)
small tin of tomatoes
500 ml water or vegetable stock
salt & pepper

Chicken curry

4–6 chicken pieces
1 pinch salt
2 tablespoons oil
2 small onions
15 g curry powder
15 g flour
1 tablespoon vinegar
15 g brown sugar
25 g sultanas
100 ml coconut milk
300 ml chicken stock

Pizza

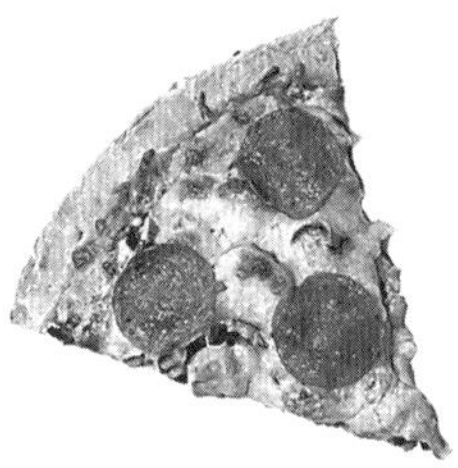

1 cup lukewarm water
2 teaspoons dry yeast
1 teaspoon sugar
1 teaspoon salt
1 tablespoon olive oil
2–3 cups plain flour
1 teaspoon cornflour
fresh tomato or pizza sauce
oregano
mozzarella cheese
pizza toppings (to taste)
e. g. ham, salami, tuna fish, olives

Dad's savoury mince

1 kg minced beef
3 tablespoons onions, cut up finely
1/2 teaspoon salt
1/4 teaspoon pepper
2 eggs
1/2 cup flour
2 tablespoons butter
2 cups beef stock

stock: a liquid made by boiling meat or vegetables, which is used to make soups
pinch: a small amount, a little
yeast: Hefe
savoury: (of a meal) not sweet
mince: to cut meat into very small pieces, usually using a machine

Mum's favourite cake

190 g dark chocolate, melted
190 g butter
190 g sugar
100 g plain flour
good pinch cinnamon (to taste)
3 eggs, beaten
pinch salt

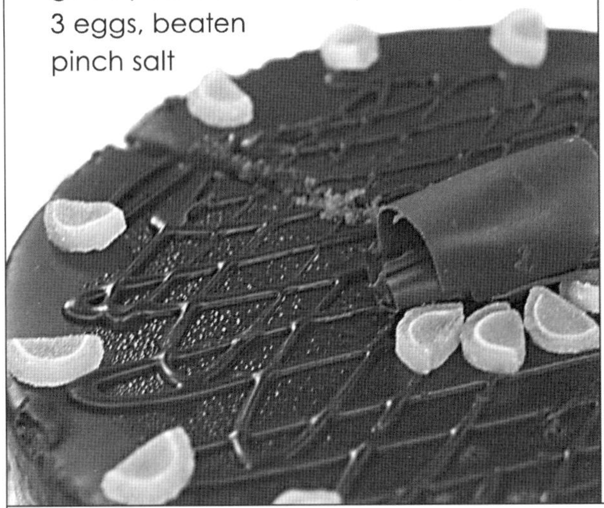

Sherry trifle

8 biscuits or small sponge cake
4 tablespoons raspberry jam
6 tablespoons sweet sherry
12 ounces frozen or fresh raspberries
nuts flaked
custard or vanilla pudding
200 g double cream
2 tablespoons sugar
2 ounces almonds,
toasted
1/2 pint milk

Californian muffins

150 g plain flour
50 g sugar
25 g milk powder
1 1/2 tablespoons baking powder
1/2 tablespoon cinnamon
1/4 tablespoon salt
125 ml vegetable oil
60 ml honey
60 ml maple syrup
2 eggs
1/2 tablespoon vanilla essence
1 large apple
75 g carrots
75 g raisins

cinnamon: Zimt
raspberry: Himbeere
ounce: 28.35 grams
pint: 0.568 litres

1 Scan the lists of ingredients and give short answers.

a How many recipes for savoury dishes has Sandra chosen? ______________________

b For which recipe(s) do they need onions?

____

c Malcolm and Pat do not like the taste of cinnamon. Which recipe(s) can they not use?

____

d Meryl has discovered that there is no yeast in the house. Which recipe(s) can they not use?

____

e Alan has offered to go to the butcher's next door. Which ingredient(s) can he buy there?

____

2 Work with your partner: Make a list of the spices the friends need.

3 Tell your partner which of these ingredients you wouldn't find in your kitchen cupboards at home.

____

____

____

____

____

____

4 In the end, each of the friends says which recipe he/she would prefer.
Can you find their favourites? Fill in the grid.

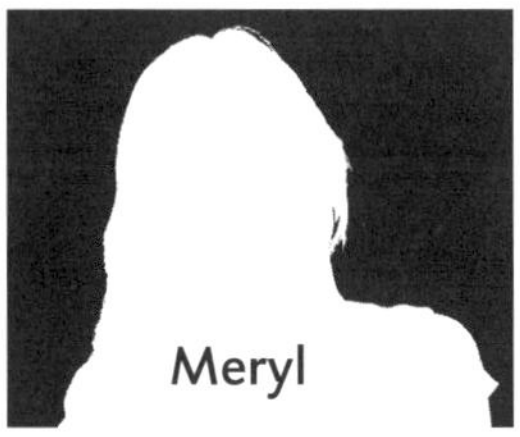

As you all know, I'm a chocolate fan, so there is only one choice for me.

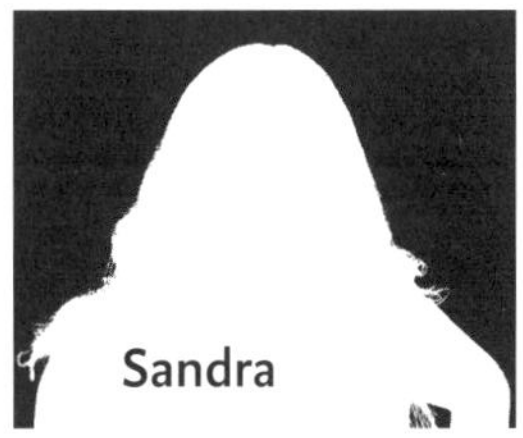

I'm not on a diet, but I don't fancy anything fattening. Best would be a nice soup.

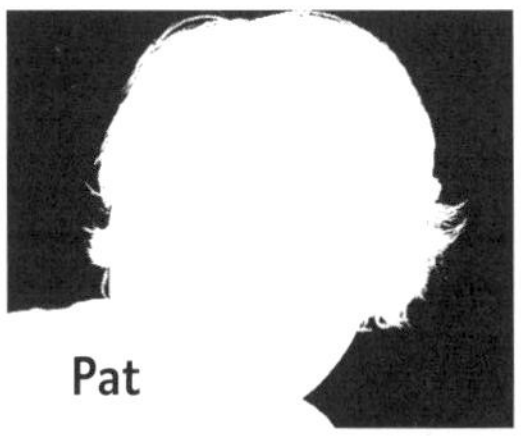

I need something to build me up. I'm quite hungry at the moment. So let's have a meaty dish.

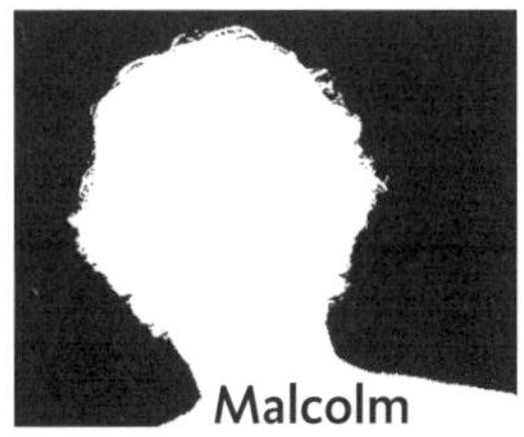

Well, friends, it's the weekend. Why not have something with a bit of alcohol in it? You don't get drunk on that!

I'd like something sweet. But I can't have anything with nuts, I'm allergic to nuts.

My favourite dish would be something exotic, not the old pizza or spaghetti. Let's make something Asian!

Meryl	Sandra	Pat	Malcolm	Linda	Alan

5 As they cannot agree on what meal to cook, the friends decide to eat out.
Draw a mind map of the food and drinks they find on the menu of the restaurant.
You can use words from the lists and add your own ideas.

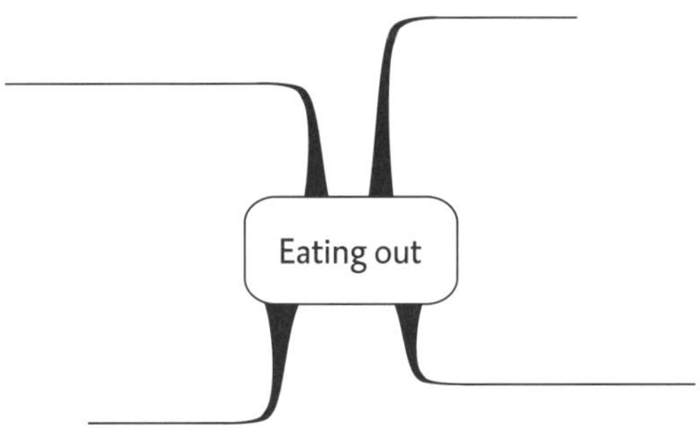

6 From theory to practice: Go to the Internet and find out how to make for example chicken curry or any other dish you would prefer.

M5 Road Safety

1 Mark words and phrases which in your opinion are important to understand the text. Use a dictionary to look up unknown words.

Tip

Close reading means to study a text carefully ...
- to understand its meaning and message.
- to understand its language (vocabulary, style, images, symbols).
- to be able to interpret it (story, poem). ■

Cinema fans will get the safety message

The Ministry of Transport will use the latest technology to warn young people of the dangers of careless driving. To improve road safety video clips of distracted drivers will be beamed directly to youngsters' mobile phones in cinemas throughout Scotland using the latest Bluetooth technology. The move was announced by Transport Minister Stewart Stevenson and it comes after research revealed that young people are less likely to use traditional media like television and are much more likely to use mobiles and the Internet. The new technology works by beaming a film clip onto the young person's phone as they arrive in cinema foyers and runs together with a new cinema advert from Road Safety Scotland which shows that momentary distraction is one of the main causes of road accidents.

Mr Stevenson said: "The latest statistics show a decrease in road accidents in Scotland in 2007, but we cannot and will not be satisfied with this development. Too many people are still dying on Scotland's roads and sadly young drivers continue to be over-represented in these deaths. As a government, we are constantly looking at new ways to reach this age group and I am determined that we look beyond the traditional and towards the innovative in our efforts to save lives. This campaign is new, and it can make a real difference. Ninety seven per cent of young people between 18 and 24 now own a mobile phone. That is a huge audience we can reach with this campaign."

The technology works by beaming an advert onto a young person's phone. Once accepted, the clip showing young people travelling in a car, is interrupted as a text message is received. After clicking the message, the clip starts again to show what happens when drivers are distracted. The message 'one distraction is all it takes' then appears.

From: http://www.falkirkherald.co.uk/news/Cinema-fans-will-get-the.4367737.jp (adapted)

2 Look at the different definitions of these words from the text. Which German definition do you think is most suitable for each word in its particular use in the text?

beam (l. 7):	**save** (l. 41):	**take** (l. 59):
n. Lichtstrahl Strahlenbündel Balken **v.** strahlen anstrahlen, anlächeln ausstrahlen senden	**n.** Abwehr (Fußball) **prep.** außer **v.** sparen, retten, schützen aufheben (für die Zukunft) sammeln sichern (Daten) verhindern (Tor)	**n.** Einnahmen Aufnahme (Film) **v.** annehmen, etw. hinbringen nehmen, ertragen, aufnehmen, brauchen, wegnehmen, stehlen, zu sich nehmen, gefangen nehmen

beam: ______________________

save: ______________________

take: ______________________

3 Answer these questions on the text in complete sentences.

a Which new technology does the Ministry of Transport use?

____

b Why does the Ministry of Transport use this technology?

____

____

c Why do most accidents happen?

____

____

4 What is the general message of the text? Tick (✓) the correct box.

☐ A video message warns teenagers of the dangers of drinking and driving.

☐ A video message tells teenagers to drive carefully.

☐ A video message tells teenagers not to use mobile phones in cinemas.

M6 Teenagers Today

Catherine Jones investigates the so-called hoodie generation.*
A recent survey found many adults were frightened of the youths that walk our streets; but what happens if you stop judging and start talking to a gang of them? Catherine Jones spoke to seven teenagers (aged 16 to 18) to discover how they feel about their "hoodie" image.

* hoodie (hoody): a sweatshirt, jacket, or other top with a hood *(Kapuze)*

REPORTER: How do you think teenagers are viewed today?

ALEX: I think people think we are all the same. If you are a teenager, you are all trouble – there are no nice teenagers. It always seems to be a negative reaction. For most of the public, what they see of teenagers is on the streets, drinking, fighting – all bad stuff. They don't see the positive side of teenagers, like them doing well in school.

MALI: If there are teenagers who give a negative image that's because they have a lot of problems – there are a lot of reasons why they are like they are. Some people might do it for image and to get noticed.

KATE: Because they are bored, because there's nothing to do.

CHRIS: There's nothing to do if you are between 16 and 18.

ALEX: And nowhere to go.

MATTHEW: Nothing else to do.

CHRIS: Because youth clubs are closed at half-term and school holidays which is just when you want them. If they were there, people would use them. People end up hanging out on the streets and then get a negative image.

half-term: a short school holiday

REPORTER: What is your attitude to politics?

ALEX: There's nothing really that interests me.

MILLEE: I don't understand it!

KATE: It's something for adults, because they have the vote.

CHRIS: If it was more for young people – like spending money for places where they can go like sports grounds – politics might interest them more.

REPORTER: How do you feel about your parents?

GRAEME: I have got a good relationship with mine. I'd go to my parents with certain problems – say like a health problem because they are more likely to know about that kind of thing but otherwise I would probably talk to friends.

ALEX: If my parents told me I couldn't go out, I'd probably go out anyway.

REPORTER: A new survey says seven out of 10 pupils in the UK have experienced bullying. Is it such a big issue for young people?

CHRIS: We don't see a lot of it in the sixth form because we are away from everyone else.

ALEX: Before GCSEs, people do pick on people but not really that much.

GCSE (General Certificate of Secondary Education): British school exam, taken by secondary school students at age 14–16

to intervene: sich einmischen

GRAEME: If it was someone you know then you'd intervene.

MATTHEW: If you're not involved then you shouldn't really get involved.

CHRIS: Stay out of it.

REPORTER: What do you regard as important in life?

MATTHEW: Going out.

MILLEE: My life is quite different because of my religion. I have been brought up as a Christian and that is the most important thing in my life. It used to be really hard and at one time I used to be embarrassed but now that's not the case.

ALEX: Football.

GRAEME: Money.

REPORTER: Where do you hope to be in 10 years time?

MILLEE: Working in the media – TV or film production.

ALEX: Don't have a clue. Maybe something to do with sport.

KATE: Something to do with medicine or sports.

CHRIS: Big house with a Porsche outside. Teaching perhaps. I can dream.

MALI: Something sports-related. I'd like to have my own gym.

GRAEME: Fire or police service. Three or four of my friends want to go into the public services.

MATTHEW: I definitely want to go through university.

REPORTER: How important is marriage?

MALI: It happens when it happens.

ALEX: I won't start looking for the right woman until I am 28.

MALI: If you look, you don't get.

MILLEE: Some day I'll meet the right one.

REPORTER: How do you feel about the state of Britain?

ALEX: A mess.

ALEX: We come from a nice part of the country but some parts of London sound pretty bad. Lots of violence. I think the country is not in a good way.

Greggs: British chain of bakeries

MALI: I know someone who got attacked here when they were getting their Greggs pie by two kids who were younger than them.

ALEX: That kind of thing happens every day in London.

MATTHEW: I come from London and all my friends have been mugged.

to mug: to attack and rob somebody

REPORTER: What's your message to the nation?

ALEX: People don't get to hear the good things about teenagers.

GRAEME: People only want to hear about the bad things. But if you meet teenagers you see they are not all bad. You do get the odd person and those few ruin it for everyone else.

From: http://www.walesonline.co.uk/news/education-news/2006/11/08/welsh-teens-the-truth-91466-18063034 (adapted)

1 Read the text and tick (✓) the correct answer.

Tip

When doing a **multiple choice** task …
- study the text carefully.
- read all questions or statements.
- return to the main text and mark your solutions. ■

a The reporter wants to know …
- [ ] why teenagers always have to wear hoodies.
- [ ] what the teenagers think about the image of young people in the eyes of the general public.
- [ ] what teenagers think about older people.

b The teenagers say that some youngsters behave badly because …
- [ ] between 16 and 18 they hate everybody.
- [ ] they feel too much under pressure.
- [ ] they don't know what to do with themselves.

c One of teenagers says …
- [ ] he always does what his parents tell him to do.
- [ ] he doesn't care what his parents tell him to do.
- [ ] he always does the opposite of what his parents tell him.

d The teenagers say about bullying that …
- [ ] it is something you should stay out of.
- [ ] it doesn't happen often in their school.
- [ ] it is very unpleasant if it happens to someone you know.

2 Answer the questions in complete sentences.

a Why are young people not interested in politics?

____

____

b What is Graeme's relationship to his parents like?

____

c What do the teenagers think about violence?

____

____

d Do you think that life in Wales is safer than in the British capital? Justify your answer.

____

3 What's on in the West End?
After their final school exams the teenagers go on a trip to London to celebrate.
They would like to go to a show in London's famous West End.
A look into the paper informs them about what's on.

a Can you find out the titles of the five shows? Fill in the blanks in the adverts with a partner.

A

____

This is a musical about a boy from the working class who grows up without a mother in the north of England. His father works in a coal mine and wants his son to take up boxing. Instead, the boy discovers a love for ballet. He goes to have secret lessons and becomes a very good dancer with the famous Royal Ballet.

Tickets: £25.50–£64.50

B

____

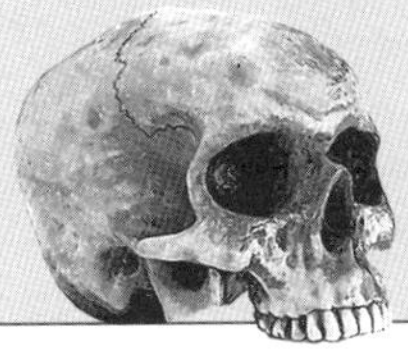

Shakespeare's famous play is a murder story. The King of Denmark is dead. His son is sure that his father was murdered. A ghost tells the Prince that his uncle Claudius, who married his mother, killed the old king. The Prince is about to lose his mind.

Starring: Jude Law

Tickets: sold out! Some return tickets may be available on the day from 10 a.m. in person from the box office.

C

____

Tchaikovsky's first ballet is one of the greatest classical ballets of all time. Its romance and beauty has fascinated people for more than 100 years. While hunting, Prince Siegfried sees an amazing swan. As he takes aim to shoot, the swan turns into a beautiful woman.

Tickets: £35.50–£84.50

D

____

A group of people spend a weekend in the countryside. They discover there is a murderer among them. The question is which one of them is the killer? This play by the British "Queen of Crime" is the longest-running show in London. It opened in 1952. Since then more than 23,000 performances have been given.

Tickets: £20.00–£59.00

E

____

This tragedy is the classical love story. Two teenagers meet at a party in Verona and fall in love, but the problem is that their families are bitter enemies. It seems their love is doomed before it can start.

Tickets: £25.50–£75.50

b This is what some of the boys and girls would like to see. Who would choose which performance? Fill in the grid below.

1 Jamie

Well, I'm not too keen on culture and I don't mind what we are going to see. I know that London tickets are expensive, but I don't want to spend more than £ 20. I'd rather spend my money in a disco.

2 Josh

I would like to see one of the classics. Because in London you always get top actors. I know it's expensive and sometimes difficult to get tickets. I'm prepared to pay more, but I don't want to queue in front of the theatre in the morning.

3 Megan

I've been to a West End theatre before. My parents took me to see a play with Harry Potter star Daniel Radcliffe. There is always a play on with a big film star in it. I'd like to see that again. I don't mind what sort of play it is.

4 Lucy

When I was a little girl I had ballet lessons. I don't do ballet any more, but I'm still interested in dancing. I'd like to see some real professionals on stage.

5 Luke

I'm more for entertainment. None of that heavy stuff with old-fashioned language which nobody understands. A detective story would interest me.

A	B	C	D	E

4 Which performance would you like to go to? Give reasons.
Work in five groups and collect arguments for and against each show.
Use the Internet to find out more about the contents of the shows.
Choose a speaker for your team who will give a short presentation of your results.
Then hold a discussion in class and decide where you would like to go together.
Can you reach a compromise?
You can use this table to collect the most important arguments for and against each production and to note down the number of pupils who are in favour of each event.

Show	For	Against
A	number of pupils:	
B	number of pupils:	
C	number of pupils:	
D	number of pupils:	
E	number of pupils:	

5 Where to stay: Go to page 4 and find the youth hostel which would be best for the teenagers to stay.

The best hostel would be: ______________________ Reason: ______________________

6 How to get there: In the end, as none of the five shows suited all of them, the group managed to get half-price tickets for the musical *Jersey Boys* in the Prince Edward Theatre.
Using a London street map on the Internet they looked up how to get to the theatre.

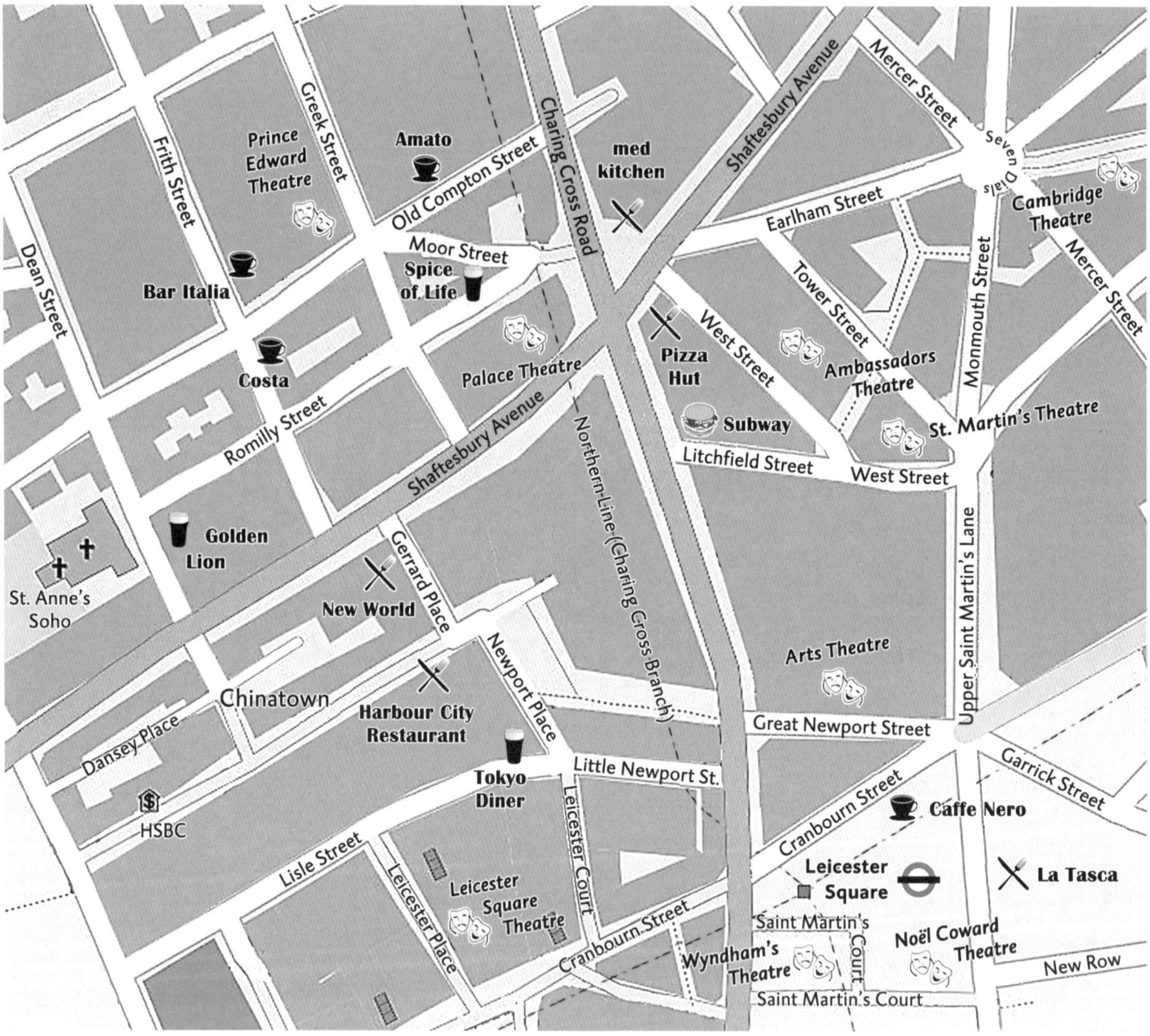

a Work with a partner. Tell him/her how to get from Leicester Square tube station to the Prince Edward Theatre in Old Compton Street.

b Work in groups and imagine the following situations:
- After the show the boys want to go to a pub for a drink (non-alcoholic, of course, for those who are under 18), whereas the girls would prefer tea or hot chocolate. They ask one of the theatre staff where they could go. Write down the dialogue and act it out in front of the class.
- Later on, the girls join the boys in the pub. When it's time to get back to the youth hostel they ask the publican how to get to Leicester Square tube station. What does he say?

M7 Do Something Funny for Money

His job is making people laugh. New Zealander Richard Curtis wrote funny sketches for British comedian Rowan Atkinson *(Mr Bean)* and scripts for the successful film comedies *Four Weddings and a Funeral, Notting Hill* and *Bridget Jones.* However, he himself was very sad and shocked about the hundreds and thousands of people who died of hunger in Eritrea and Ethiopia. Curtis felt that something had to be done. In 1985 he turned to some friends from the film and music industry for help and took up an idea of charity worker Jane Tewson to form an organization called Comic Relief. Its aim was to collect money in order to help people survive in poor countries. At about the same time the Irish singer Bob Geldof had formed a charity organization called BandAid to collect money for the fight against hunger in Africa.

charity: Wohltätigkeits-

When it first started, Comic Relief concentrated its help on the African country Ethiopia and its southern neighbour Eritrea because both belong to the world's poorest nations. In both countries farming is difficult because the earth is of very poor quality and the climate is extremely dry. Constant wars have made the situation worse. As a result, both countries cannot produce enough food and many people die of hunger. As buying food on the world market is expensive, the charity organizations help to finance food imports. Today Comic Relief also supports poor families not only in Africa but also in Britain.

Bob Geldof and his friends arrange concerts and sell records (e.g. *Do They Know It's Christmas?*) to collect money. Comic Relief has developed its very own way to raise funds. Every two years in the spring the charity organizes Red Nose Day, which has become a very special day in Britain. School children do not have to wear uniforms, and instead of having lessons they work on special projects. People all over the country wear a red plastic nose like clowns and organize events in support of Comic Relief. Politicians, popular TV personalities, famous artists and film stars, members of clubs and churches, shopkeepers, office and bank clerks – just about everybody arranges some sort of funny or spectacular project. Some activities are rather traditional, others unusual and spectacular. Some people bake and sell cakes, others organize fashion shows, supermarkets sell special wines (Red Nose Red and Red Nose White), actors and ballet dancers wear red noses and costumes at special performances, a vicar even illuminated one tower of his church red to attract attention to the good cause of Comic Relief. In 2009, nine celebrities successfully climbed Mount Kilimanjaro and raised over one and a half million pounds. On Red Nose Day all of these people take part in activities to show that they care about others. All through the day BBC television reports on the activities planned across the country and shows on a scale how much money has already been collected for projects in the UK and Africa. Since its beginning in 1985 Comic Relief has raised more than £600 million. Richard Curtis received a special TV award for his charity work.

1 Decide whether the following statements are true, false or not in the text. Tick (✓) the correct box.

	true	false	not in the text
Richard Curtis comes from Africa.	☐	☐	☐
Jane Tewson first had the idea for Comic Relief.	☐	☐	☐
Bob Geldof founded Comic Relief.	☐	☐	☐
Hunger is a big problem in Africa.	☐	☐	☐
Today money from Comic Relief also goes to the UK.	☐	☐	☐
Red Nose Day takes place twice a year.	☐	☐	☐
On Red Nose Day kids do not go to school.	☐	☐	☐
On Red Nose Day people dress up like clowns.	☐	☐	☐
The more traditional events are less successful.	☐	☐	☐
Famous people raised one and a half million pounds by climbing Mount Kilimanjaro.	☐	☐	☐
The BBC plans all activities in the country.	☐	☐	☐
Germany has its own Red Nose Day every two years.	☐	☐	☐

Tip

When doing a **true/false-task** …
- study the original text carefully.
- go through the statements one by one.
- compare each statement with the information given in the text.
- mark your solution. ■

2 Find the phrases in the text which express the following German meanings:

a „etwas musste unternommen werden“

____

b „für den Kampf gegen den Hunger“

____

c „ein Pfarrer strahlte sogar einen Turm seiner Kirche rot an“

____

d „um die Aufmerksamkeit auf die gute Sache zu lenken“

____

3 Work with a partner and answer the questions on the text.
Do not copy complete sentences from the text. Use your own words as far as possible.

a Why did Richard Curtis and his friends start Comic Relief?

b Why did Comic Relief first concentrate on African countries?

c What could Comic Relief do to help Ethiopia and Eritrea?

d What is special about Red Nose Day?

e Why do you think is Red Nose Day such a success in Britain?

4 Here are some ideas of how school children can help Comic Relief on Red Nose Day to raise money. Work with a partner. Choose from these ideas and decide what you would like to do and how much money you would expect to raise. Give reasons.

QUICK AND EASY

Raising cash for Red Nose Day doesn't have to take weeks on end. In fact, it can take hardly any time at all with these fast and furious fundraising ideas. Just take your pick and raise a few bob – even a small amount of cash can make the world of difference!

SPARE SOME CHANGE

Empty your pockets, purse or wallet every day for a week and donate your small change to Red Nose Day. Encourage your friends and family to do the same and don't forget to check down the back of the sofa. Small change can make a big difference.

SWEEPSTAKE POSTER

Pin up the Red Nose Day Sweepstake Poster at work, in your club or local pub and charge everyone £ 2 to play. Order your poster here.

BUY SOME GOODIES

Choose an official RND T-shirt from the most iconic charity T-shirt range ever created and go ahead and Pick Your Nose! We've got some wonderful Red Nose Day goodies to get your mitts on!

WEAR SOMETHING FUNNY

Spend the day in your pyjamas, dress as your favourite comedy character or put your clothes on back to front. Get sponsored to do it on your own or do it en masse with colleagues or classmates and charge everyone to join in.

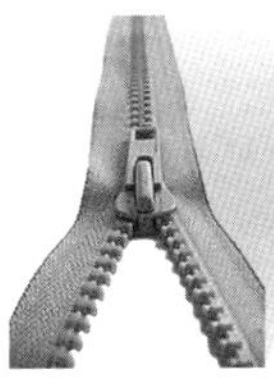

ZIP IT!

Get sponsored to keep shtum for a day. You might be surprised how much your family or colleagues will cough up in order for you to keep quiet!

WAX IT!

Your legs, your chest, your back – if it's hairy, get sponsored to get it waxed for cash.

GIVE IT UP!

Chocolate, biscuits, coffee – get sponsored to give up something you love!

From: http://www.rednoseday.com/do_something/fundraising_ideas

bob: here: money; sweepstake: a type of betting in which the winner receives all the money risked by everyone else
iconic: ikonisch, kultig; *range: a set of similar products*
mitts: a type of glove that does not have separate parts for each finger; here: to get your hand on
en masse: here: together; shtum: silent
cough up: here: to give someone money

5 A Red Nose project: This is an example of what Comic Relief does with the money which is raised.
- Look up words and expressions which you do not understand in a dictionary.
- Write a few sentences about how Comic Relief can help children and their families with the money that is collected. Try to use your own words as far as possible.

HELP CHILDREN WHO CARE FOR THEIR FAMILIES

RED NOSE DAY

Choice cards – secondary

Help children who have to care for their families

When was the last time you were sick? Or your parent or guardian was unwell and you had to do your bit to look after them or the house? This happens all over the world to families everyday and is no different for millions of families across Africa.
But in Africa, people are much more vulnerable to illness because of the climate and diseases found in tropical areas, poverty and HIV. When poor people get ill, it takes them much longer to get better as their bodies are often too weak to fight the infection.

The following list increases a person's chances of not recovering from illness quickly:
- No easy access to a doctor or regular access to immunisation
- Housing that is basic and cramped
- Not having safe drinking water within easy reach
- Poor diet

When people living in these conditions become HIV-positive their outlook is generally not good.

HIV and the individual

A person who is HIV-positive could live for a long time. There are plenty of examples of HIV-positive people in richer countries across Europe, in the US and in countries in Africa, who continue to live healthy and productive lives. This is because they have access to healthcare, personal support and can look after themselves well.
However, in the majority of African countries, when a person becomes HIV-positive it is usually against a backdrop of poverty and hardship. Unless they can afford the medicines and are able to eat well, their quality of life will be poor. When this happens it's easier to pick other illnesses, such as TB, and these can weaken the body significantly.
The effect on families is devastating.

Form: http://www.rednoseday.com/files/rnd09/assets/resource_bank/Choice_Card_Secondary_-_Care_For_Families_FINAL.pdf (September 2009)

M8 Going West – Part 1

In 1843 Paddy O'Hearne, 36, and his wife Molly, 32, left their small farm in Leinster, Ireland, because the potato crops had failed three years running. With their two boys Adam, 12, and Luke, 10, they emigrated to the New World, to join Molly's brother Frank, who had left Ireland ten years earlier and had set up a farm in Kentucky. (**1**) For the next couple of years Paddy and Luke worked on Frank's farm, and Adam helped in Mr Wilson's hardware store in the town. After a while Paddy O'Hearne became rather restless: He wanted to work his own land again. Not in the neighbourhood, but thousands of miles away in the Far West in California or Oregon where there was plenty of free farmland for all.

crop: plants grown on a farm (= harvest)

One of his neighbours, Josh Kennedy wanted to try his luck in California, because he had heard news of gold finds in the Sacramento area. Paddy told his wife about his idea to move into the West. (**2**) On Christmas Day 1849, Amy, their fourth child, was born, and Molly eventually gave in to her husband's and their boys' pleadings and agreed to join a wagon train which was to set out for California and Oregon in April or May of the coming year from Independence, Missouri. The boys were excited and looking forward to the adventure.

to plead: to ask in a serious way

In March 1850, the O'Hearne and Kennedy families arrived in Independence, their starting point on the way west. During most of the year Independence was a rather small and quiet town on the Missouri River, but every year in spring large numbers of emigrants gathered in camps to prepare for the long journey to California or Oregon. In 1843 more than a thousand pioneers had first opened up the Oregon Trail from Independence, making it one of the favourite "jumping off" places. (**3**) So the emigrants waited for the grass to grow in the prairie on which their oxen, which pulled the wagons, could graze. With the financial help from Molly's brother Frank and Adam's employer, Mr Wilson, Paddy was able to buy the necessary equipment – mainly farming and household tools – and food for the journey. The wagon train, which Paddy and Josh had decided to join, was to be led by Captain Shadrack, who informed all emigrants to provide themselves above all with flour, bacon, coffee, sugar and salt.

to gather: to come together in one place

In May the words "The grass is up!" rang through the camp and it was time to go. Many wagons started at the same time, trying to push ahead to find the best place, and Captain Shadrack and his helpers had a job to avoid a traffic jam, but eventually everything went well. The first part of the journey, which followed the Platte River west, was not too bad – the land was flat, the grass was green, the water fresh –

but Molly and the baby began to suffer as the days became hotter. Every morning Paddy, the boys and all the men got up early, around 4 or 5, to get the wagons ready, and after breakfast the march began. At midday, they stopped for a short rest and a meal, before the march continued again. **(4)** The men went hunting for antelopes or buffalo, the children looked for fire wood and brought water so that the women could make dinner and prepare the lunch for the next day. It was hard work for everyone. Each day passed much like any other, and Molly felt rather lonely, but she was too exhausted to complain.

1 Read lines 1–19 and decide whether the following statements are true, false or not in the text. Tick (✓) the correct answer.

	true	false	not in the text
Paddy left Ireland because he wanted to find gold in the New World.	☐	☐	☐
Paddy and his brother Frank left Ireland together and set up a farm in Kentucky.	☐	☐	☐
Adam O'Hearne wanted to become an engineer.	☐	☐	☐
After Amy was born Molly agreed to go West.	☐	☐	☐
The wagon train started from Kentucky.	☐	☐	☐

2 Read lines 20–34 and write down the passages from the text which tell you …

a that Independence was not a busy place.

____

b why Paddy could afford to buy all the tools and the food for the journey.

____

____

c why the settlers knew what they had to pack into their wagons.

____

____

____

3 Work with a partner. From the box choose a suitable heading for each paragraph.
There is one heading which you do not need to use.
Write the correct headings on the lines above the paragraphs.

An adventurous plan – An easy start – Leaving home – Marching through the desert – Preparing for the trek

4 Work with a partner and read the text again. Four sentences have been removed from Part 1. Choose from the sentences (A–E) the one which fits each gap (1–4). Write the correct number of the gap behind each sentence. There is one sentence which you do not need to use.

- A They travelled until sunset, when they set up camp for the night. ☐
- B Because of the heavy snowfall they could hardly see where they were going. ☐
- C But Molly didn't want to go on a journey which would last for months – especially as she was pregnant again. ☐
- D Shortly after their arrival their third child, Laura, was born. ☐
- E The journey to the Far West could only be made during the summer months and before the first snowfall. ☐

5 Answer these questions in your own words as far as possible.

a What did the O'Hearne family do after they arrived in Kentucky?

____

____

b Why did Josh Kennedy want to go to California?

____

c Why did the pioneers have to wait for the grass to grow in the prairie?

____

____

d Why was the first part of the long journey easy?

____

____

M9 Going West – Part 2

In June, the heat increased and people and wagons often disappeared in clouds of dust. The grass was getting drier and very often the boys could not find any wood, so that buffalo dung was used to light a fire. When it rained for days, the wagons got stuck in the mud and the trail was almost impassable. Although the canvas of the wagon had been treated with oil to protect it from the rain, the water still came through and made everything wet inside. Valuable food began to rot. Many people realised that they had overloaded their wagons and had to throw furniture, stoves and heavy equipment overboard. One morning, Adam and Luke saw their first Native Americans. They had been told some wild stories about the Indians, but soon learned they were friendly people, helping the settlers to cross rivers, to unload and reload wagons. One day Adam almost drowned, but he was rescued by two Indian boys. As a reward for their help the Native Americans were given tools and clothes. Only later, when more and more pioneers passed through Indian territory, killing off many buffalos, Indians did begin to attack wagon trains.

impassable: impossible to cross

stove: an apparatus for cooking or heating food (= cooker, oven)

to drown: to die under water because of not getting enough air

Several people, among them baby Amy, fell seriously ill, but could not be treated because there was no doctor. Paddy and others wanted to rest for a day or two at the next Fort, but many complained about the slow pace of march and wanted to push on faster in order to cross the South Pass in the Rocky Mountains before the first snowfall. Luckily, baby Amy soon recovered, but a number of people died and had to be buried. One out of ten emigrants did not survive the journey and died in accidents, from cholera and other diseases. The mountainous roads made travelling difficult, and the nights were very cold. Arguments between Captain Shadrack and Mr Judd's group about the choice of campsites and the number of guards to post for the night led to Mr Judd and ten wagons, the rebels, leaving the trek and pushing on alone.

pace: speed

After months of strenuous travelling Captain Shadrack's trek eventually reached Fort Hall on the Snake River in Idaho. After two days rest at the Fort, the Kennedys and the O'Hearnes said good-bye to each other, with the Kennedy family joining travellers bound for California. Paddy, Molly and their children finished the rest of their journey taking a further three months before arriving in Oregon, the land of their dreams, in October. For six months they had travelled sixteen hours almost every day, from dawn to dusk. They thanked God for having protected them and so enabling them to make their dream of a new life and a new start come true.

from dawn to dusk: from early in the morning till late at night

to enable: to make possible

1 Find headings for the paragraphs and write them on the lines.

2 Combine the matching parts of the sentences. Write the correct numbers into the grid.

A On hot and dry days the settlers could not see far ...
B The track was deep and muddy ...
C The settlers did everything to keep the rain out ...
D The early settlers were surprised ...
E Only strong and healthy pioneers survived ...
F Sometimes arguments broke out ...

1 ... because they found the Indians friendly and helpful.
2 ... because the settlers often did not have doctors.
3 ... because it had rained so heavily.
4 ... because people had different opinions.
5 ... because the trail was so dusty.
6 ... because it would ruin their food.

A	B	C	D	E	F

3 Work with a partner. Complete these sentences according to the information in the text.

a When the boys could not find any ________________, the people used ________________ to make a fire.

b Before the settlers could ________________ a river, they had to ________________ their wagons.

c On later treks, the whites ________________ too many buffalo, so that the Indians began to ________________ the pioneers.

d Mr Judd and his group ________________ the trek, because they wanted to carry on ________________.

4 Go through both parts of the text *Going West* again and try to complete this mind map.

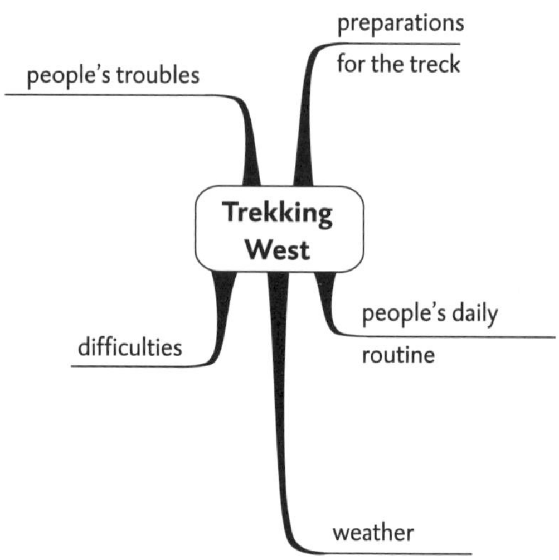

5 Work with a partner and imagine you meet Luke and Adam.
Ask them four questions to find out more about their adventure.
Then try to answer your partner's questions from Luke and Adam's perspective.

Questions	Your partner's answers

M10 The Lord from the Poor Side of Town

He was born in a poor family in the East End of London and made it to the top, becoming a multi-millionaire, a Lord and a TV star. Alan Michael Sugar, born in 1947, is one of those men who made it 'from rags to riches'. His life wasn't a success story from the beginning. Alan, whose father was a tailor, left school without any qualifications when he was 16 and joined the civil service. He did not like his work there; he wanted to be self-employed, and therefore started his own business. From his savings of £100 he bought a van which he used as his "shop", selling cigarette lighters, car aerials and other small electrical equipment. At 21 Alan Michael Sugar founded a firm which he called Amstrad – a combination of the first letters of his name and the word 'trading' – dealing in stereo and TV sets.

rag: a small piece of cloth that is usually used for cleaning

aerial: a radio or television antenna

Amstrad was very successful, doubling its profit every year. As Alan Sugar had a special talent for sensing new developments, he entered the home computer market in the early 1980s. Within eight years Amstrad sold more than three million units of its computer models, mainly because Sugar's PCs were cheaper and technically up to date. There seemed to be no end to the firm's success story, but trouble came in the 1990s. Using a faulty hard disk for its computers Amstrad PCs earned themselves a bad name and eventually the company lost many customers. The firm recovered from the failure however, when Britain's new pay TV company "Sky" chose Amstrad as the manufacturer of its set top box which viewers needed to receive Sky TV channels.

faulty: bad, not working well

Coming from a working class background Alan Sugar had always been interested in football. In 1991 he bought London's famous football club Tottenham Hotspur F.C. and became its chairman for nine years. It wasn't a happy time, though. One of the disappointments concerned the German football star Jürgen Klinsmann. In 1994/95 Klinsmann played such a brilliant season for Sugar's club that he was voted England's Player of the Year. In spite of this achievement Klinsmann refused to renew his contract for another season because he wanted to return to Germany to join Bayern Munich. Alan Sugar was so furious that during a TV interview he threw Jürgen Klinsmann's shirt away. After ten years Sugar left Tottenham, saying that the time with the club had been a waste and had cost him a lot of money. However, he did not stay at home, relaxing and enjoying the profits which he earned from the property he had bought in London's fashionable district Mayfair. Alan Sugar started his third career as host of the BBC show *The Apprentice*.

chairman: a man who is the boss of a club or firm

fashionable: modern, popular, expensive

The programme tests the business skills of the candidates and is different from other reality shows. Viewers do not vote for a winner – Alan Sugar is the boss. He chooses tasks for two teams and he decides on the winner. The prize is real: the best candidate receives a contract in one of Sugar's companies. The boss wants to make sure that the show is not just a game, but has a serious background, giving insight into the world of work, so he also suggested a young version of the show, *Junior Apprentice*. He said, "It is my belief that we should be doing more to help young people understand how businesses work, because the future of our economy relies on them. I believe that the key to business success lies in hard work and common sense and that we should encourage our young people as much as possible." Young candidates – five boys and five girls aged between 16 and 17 – from all social backgrounds have to prove their business talent. It is obvious that these young people do not have any business experience, but the main idea is that they – and the young viewers – are introduced to the world of work. As in the original show, nine of the contestants have to leave, one by one over the weeks, with Sir Alan's phrase "you're fired" marking the end of their TV appearance.

contestant: someone who takes part in a competition or a show

---

Not everybody liked the way Alan Sugar treated people on the show. His outwardly rough and direct manner raised criticism, with some people even accusing him of bullying. One critic described Sugar as bad-tempered and exclaimed, "Why on earth would anyone want to work for Sir Alan Sugar?" Others were worried about the fact that the winner was only judged by the profit he managed to make. Success by any means and greed should not be the only aim in the real world. However, others say Alan Sugar might seem rough and unfeeling on the surface, but in real life he is an open, honest and also caring person. He gives a lot of his money to charities, because he does not forget where he came from: the poor East End of London.

bad-tempered: angry, in a bad mood

1 Choose the correct headings for the paragraphs. There is one headline which you don't need. Write the headlines on the lines above the paragraphs.

Winning the championship
In the firing line
Rising to star fame
An early start after school
Selling and earning millions
Years of frustration

2 Read the first two paragraphs of the text again. Which text passage tells you …

a that Alan Sugar did not take any school-leaving exams?

______

b that he had difficulties when he began his work?

______

c how Alan Sugar found the name for his firm?

______

d that he had a good feeling of what products would be needed in future?

______

e that Sugar's firm was not always successful?

______

3 Tick (✓) the correct box to complete the following sentences.

a Alan Sugar was disappointed because …
- [ ] Jürgen Klinsmann did not play well.
- [ ] he did not like the German player.
- [ ] Klinsmann did not want to stay in England.
- [ ] Klinsmann wanted more money.

b After his time with Tottenham, Alan Sugar …
- [ ] was so disappointed that he retired from all his businesses.
- [ ] began to work in television.
- [ ] began to buy property in London.
- [ ] counted his profits from the club management.

c *The Apprentice* …
- [ ] is a new game show.
- [ ] is a programme in which TV viewers choose the winner.
- [ ] tests if candidates are good singers.
- [ ] offers candidates a chance to start work for Alan Sugar.

d Some people criticize Alan Sugar because ...

☐ he is so aggressive.
☐ he sets difficult tasks.
☐ he is the only person to decide on the winner.
☐ his tasks have nothing to do with real life.

4 Make a list with arguments for and against the TV show *Junior Apprentice.* Then start a discussion in groups.

5 Read the text about reality TV and do the tasks below.

Reality TV

In the late 1990s, television companies, in particular in the USA, began to develop a new type of programme which they called reality TV. Once a programme was successfully tested in the USA, it was exported to TV companies in other countries which produced their national version. That is why there was or still is an English, an Indian, a German version of the original *America's Next Top Model.*

One of the earliest and heavily criticised reality TV shows was called *Big Brother.* Critics say that these programmes have nothing to do with reality, that is, real life. On the contrary, the situations are worked out and arranged by TV producers. The show *I'm a Celebrity – Get me out of Here!* for example places former stars in a studio jungle equipped with lots of TV cameras, where the participants have to cope with snakes, spiders and other horrible creatures.

The programmes which viewers watch are often recorded and edited, and therefore do not mirror real life. The aim of the TV bosses is to attract a large audience and earn money from the telephone calls of viewers who phone in to vote for or against a certain candidate.

In some of the so-called reality shows people have to compete to win a prize, for example *America's/Germany's Next Top Model.* The British television show *Britain's Got Talent* was the beginning of the careers of singers Paul Potts and Susan Boyle. In other shows people have to prove they have special skills, for example business skills. The most successful programmes of this sort in Britain is *The Apprentice.*

a Decide whether the following statements are true, false or not in the text. Tick (✓) the correct box.

	true	false	not in the text
Reality TV shows are mainly an American invention.	☐	☐	☐
TV stations in other countries adapt the American version.	☐	☐	☐
The show *Big Brother* was developed in the Netherlands.	☐	☐	☐
Viewers can phone in, but the TV bosses decide on the winner.	☐	☐	☐
Paul Potts and Susanne Boyle won first prizes in *The Appprentice.*	☐	☐	☐

b Finish the following sentences using the information from the text about reality TV.

- When a show is popular in the United States, ______________________

- When *Big Brother* was first shown on TV, ______________________
- The term "reality show" is wrong, because ______________________
- The TV companies want many viewers to phone in, because ______________________

c Work with a partner. Imagine your partner has decided to take part in a talent show on TV and wants you to apply for it, too. Try to convince him/her not to do it.
Before you start, collect arguments for and against taking part in reality TV shows.
You can swap roles or change the type of reality TV show after five minutes.

Yes, I would take part, because …	No, I wouldn't take part, because …
• ______	• ______
• ______	• ______
• ______	• ______
• ______	• ______
• ______	• ______
• ______	• ______
• ______	• ______

6 Work experience – work placements

a Read the text on work placements and write these words in their proper places:

holidays applying suit cash useful career experience earn Saturday time websites

VOLUNTARY WORK PLACEMENTS

You may have already done some work ______________, but doing a further placement while you are at school can be ______________ in your career planning.

Why do a voluntary work placement?

Work placements give you …

- a chance to find out more about a ______________ you are considering.
- some practical experience and talking to people who already do the job.
- a better idea of whether it would ______________ you.
- a better chance of standing out when ______________ for courses and jobs.

How long do work placements last?

- Many work placements involve working full-time for a fixed ______________, usually six to twelve weeks – but they're often timed to fit in with school ______________.

How to find a work placement

- Check national newspapers, especially the ______________ editions. Many organisations advertise placements at different times of the year.
- Look up the ______________ of firms.
- If you're currently at school, ask the careers office whether they can help you find a placement.
- You may also contact organisations directly, even if they are not advertising.

Remember: A work placement generally does not ______________ you much money – more than once you do not earn anything at all. But work experience can be more valuable than ______________.

b Here are five job offers (A–E) and six young people who would like to take up a work trial. Try to find the suitable offer for each person. There is one person more than there are offers, but all of them will get a placement in the end. Fill in the grid.

A

LONDON ZOO

We have 15 places for pupils in year 10 and 11 at school, and 15 places to students in further education. You have the opportunity to work along with experienced keepers and learn skills in basic animal care.
Main tasks include cleaning and maintaining animal enclosures, food preparation and feeding of the animals.
The work is physically hard, so trainees will need to be fit and healthy.

B

BBC SHEPHERDS BUSH

The BBC offers placements for pupils aged 14 and above. We're looking for applicants who are interested in a career as camera operators, sound and vision mixers and electricians. In addition, we can offer a day in our News studio, but we cannot provide time on Outside Broadcasts due to safety reasons.

You must enjoy working in a team and be very enthusiastic about working here.

C

HIGH HILL HOTEL GREENFORD

For many years our hotel has been working to provide excellent quality. We provide a first class service for our guests from the UK and overseas. A placement with us gives applicants the chance to gain work experience in the running of a hotel.
Your work area: support of our kitchen, cleaning and gardening staff.
For applicants who wish to work in reception, a foreign language (preferably French or German) is required.

D

BIG FOOD RESTAURANT EALING

Roll up your sleeves at Big Food. We offer a 10-day work experience programme for pupils of all abilities and backgrounds (minimum age 14). The placements are designed to support you in your choice of a career in catering. If you don't mind a lively working atmosphere, this is your chance to see for yourself how you can cope with our high standards of friendly and efficient service, hygiene and cleanliness.

You must be prepared to work shifts (no night shifts).

E

SUNRISE SCHOOL MIDDLESEX

We offer work placements at our school for children with special needs. Pupils interested in a career in care or medical services are given the opportunity to gain insight into working with mentally or physically challenged children (ages between 5 and 10).
After accompanying our trained staff you will be given specific tasks to do with individual children (small groups of up to three).
Applicants are expected to work for 28 hours a week.

Jeff

Ever since I got a camcorder for my birthday, I have been enthusiastic about video editing. I'd like to make my own films one day. I hope to find a work placement in the media industry.

Chris

I'm an outdoor person. I can't imagine working in an office. So, if there is anything on offer where you can work in the open air, I'll take it.

Emily

My grandparents have a guesthouse in Stratford-upon-Avon. They have many guests who come regularly to see one of the many theatre performances in the summer. I've helped there before from time to time and have enjoyed the work. I would now like to get some experience in a bigger house.

Seth

My ideal work placement would be something where I can help people. My mother is a nurse, and I think this is a rewarding job, although my mum is often tired. I would like to find out if I have the patience.

Sarah

You might laugh, but I'm looking for something exciting, I mean, it shouldn't be boring stuff. I like action, and I can work hard, I think. Even if the job is a bit stressful, I'd give it a try.

Lily

I just love animals. We have a small zoo at home with three dogs, two parakeets, a cat and a gecko. I would like to learn more about the professional care of animals – especially exotic animals. Something to do with sports would also be great as I go running at least three times a week.

Jeff	Chris	Emily	Seth	Sarah	Lily

M11 It's Back to School

US President Barack Obama speaks to young people at the beginning of the new school year.

Part 1

Jazmin Perez from Roma, Texas, didn't speak English when she first started school. Hardly anyone in her hometown went to college, and neither of her parents had gone either. But she worked hard, earned good grades, got a scholarship to Brown University, and is now in graduate school, studying public health, on her way to being Dr. Jazmin Perez.

I'm thinking about Andoni Schultz, from Los Altos, California, who's fought brain cancer since he was three. He's endured all sorts of treatments and surgeries, one of which affected his memory, so it took him much longer – hundreds of extra hours – to do his schoolwork. But he never fell behind, and he's headed to college this fall.

to endure: to be in a difficult situation for a long time without complaining

surgery: operation

fall (AE): autumn (BE)

And then there's Shantell Steve, from my hometown of Chicago, Illinois. Even when bouncing from foster home to foster home in the toughest neighborhoods, she managed to get a job at a local health center; start a program to keep young people out of gangs; and she's on track to graduate high school with honors and go on to college.

to bounce: jump, spring

foster home: not one's real parents

Jazmin, Andoni and Shantell aren't any different from any of you. They faced challenges in their lives just like you do. But they refused to give up. They chose to take responsibility for their education and set goals for themselves. And I expect all of you to do the same. [...]

Part 2

Whatever you resolve to do, I want you to commit to it. I want you to really work at it.

to resolve: decide

to commit to sth.: to work hard; to spend as much time as possible

I know that sometimes, you get the sense from TV that you can be rich and successful without any hard work – that your ticket to success is through rapping or basketball or being a reality TV star, when chances are, you're not going to be any of those things.

But the truth is, being successful is hard. You won't love every subject you study. (**1**) Not every homework assignment will seem completely relevant to your life right this minute. And you won't necessarily succeed at everything the first time you try.

That's OK. (**2**) J.K. Rowling's first *Harry Potter* book was rejected twelve times before it was finally published. Michael Jordan was cut from his high school basketball team, and he lost hundreds of games and missed thousands of shots during his career. But he once said, "I have failed over and over and over again in my life. And that is why I succeed."

These people succeeded because they understand that you can't let your failures define you – you have to let them teach you. (**3**) If you get in trouble, that doesn't mean you're a troublemaker, it means you need to try harder to behave. If you get a bad grade, that doesn't mean you're stupid, it just means you need to spend more time studying.

No one's born being good at things, you become good at things through hard work. You're not a varsity athlete the first time you play a new sport. (**4**) You've got to practice. It's the same with your schoolwork. You might have to do a math problem a few times before you get it right, or read something a few times before you understand it, or do a few drafts of a paper before it's good enough to hand in.

varsity: the main team that represents a university or school in a sport

draft: a rough piece of writing that needs more work; a sketch

Arlington, Virginia, September 8, 2009
From: http://www.whitehouse.gov/MediaResources/PreparedSchoolRemarks

1 Read Part 1 and decide whether these statements are true or false according to the text.
Tick (✓) the correct box.

	true	false
Jasmin was the first in her family to go to college.	☐	☐
Mr and Mrs Perez had to pay for their daughter's university education.	☐	☐
Adoni needed more time to do his schoolwork because he had been seriously ill.	☐	☐
He couldn't remember things very well, because he had fallen on his head as a baby.	☐	☐
Shantell is the manager of a local shop.	☐	☐
President Obama tells the story of these three people because they are very special cases.	☐	☐

2 Five sentences have been removed from Part 2.
Choose from the sentences below the one which fits each gap (1–4).
Write the correct number of the gap behind each sentence.
There is one sentence which you do not need to use.

Some of the most successful people in the world are the ones who've had the most failures.	☐
Therefore I say, look around you and care for people in need.	☐
You don't hit every note the first time you sing a song.	☐
You have to let them show you what to do differently next time.	☐
You won't click with every teacher.	☐

LÖSUNGSHEFT

Bildungsstandards Englisch
Reading

Mittlerer Schulabschluss · B1

STARK

www.stark-verlag.de
1. Auflage 2010

Arbeitstechniken und Aufgabenformate

Folgende Aufstellung ermöglicht einen schnellen Überblick über auftretende Aufgabenformate und die dazu nötigen Arbeitstechniken.
Es sind hier jeweils nur die im Fokus stehenden Fertigkeiten angegeben.

Text Type/ Task		Arbeitstechniken	Aufgabenformate
M 1 Riddle		close reading	matching (questions – answers)
M 2 Advert	**1**	skimming; finding out the type of text	short answers
	2	skimming; reading for gist	short answers
M 3 Website	**1**	scanning	table completion
	2	scanning	short answers
	3	finding further information	collecting arguments, discussion
M 4 Recipe	**1**	scanning	short answers
	2	scanning	making a list
	3	reporting/informing	making a list
	4	scanning	multiple matching (texts)
	5	structuring a word field	mind mapping
	6	finding further information	Internet research
M 5 News Article	**1**	close reading	highlighting key words, working with a dictionary
	2	scanning, close reading	choosing the correct definition
	3	close reading	answering in complete sentences
	4	close reading	multiple choice
M 6 Interview, Advert, Map	**1**	close reading	multiple choice
	2	close reading	answering in complete sentences
	3 a	finding further information	finding titles

	b	close reading	multiple matching (texts)
	4	finding information	Internet research, collecting arguments, discussion
	5	scanning	short answers
	6	reading maps	asking the way, giving information
M 7 News Article	1	close reading	true, false, not in the text
	2	scanning	finding phrases in the text which express the given German meanings
	3	close reading	answering in complete sentences
	4	planning, working out a strategy	collecting ideas, discussion
	5	close reading	working with a dictionary, answering in complete sentences
M 8 Narrative Text	1	close reading	true, false, not in the text
	2	scanning	finding phrases in the text that correspond to given paraphrases
	3	close reading	multiple matching (paragraphs – headings)
	4	scanning, close reading	multiple matching (gaps in the text – missing sentences)
	5	close reading	answering in complete sentences
M 9 Narrative Text	1	close reading	finding headings for each paragraph
	2	scanning	matching (sentence halves)
	3	scanning	sentence completion
	4	structuring a word field	mind mapping
	5	close reading, creative task	finding questions and answers
M 10 News Article, Job Offer	1	close reading	multiple matching (paragraphs – headings)
	2	scanning	finding phrases in the text that correspond to given paraphrases
	3	close reading	multiple choice

	4	finding further information	collecting arguments, discussion
	5 a	close reading	true, false, not in the text
	b	scanning	sentence completion
	c	creative task	collecting arguments, role play
	6 a	close reading	filling gaps
	b	close reading	multiple matching (texts)

M 11 Speech	1	close reading	true, false
	2	scanning, close reading	multiple matching (gaps in the text – missing sentences)
	3	scanning	finding phrases in the text that correspond to given paraphrases
	4	close reading	sequencing
	5	close reading	matching (sentence halves)
	6	close reading	answering in complete sentences

Lösungen

M1 Finding the Punch Line

A	B	C	D	E	F	G	H	I	J	K	L	M
8	6	7	11	4	2	1	10	12	9	13	5	3

M2 British Breaks

1 It's a *travel advert*.

- Elements that help you find out the type of text on the next page: photos, layout and structure (words in bold print, words in bigger font size, paragraphs)
- Elements that help you find out the type of text in general: layout: illustrative elements (photos, drawings, symbols), headings, caption *(= Untertitel)*, byline *(= Zeile in einem Zeitungsartikel mit dem Namen des Verfassers)*, words in bold print, font size, paragraphs

2 The advert was placed by a travel agency which offers eight short trips to England and Scotland. It informs about …

- where people can go.
- how long each trip lasts.
- type of room and board *(Verpflegung)*.
- how much it will cost.

M3 Youth Hostels in London

1

	London Central	Oxford Street	St. Pancras
Number of beds	*124*	*94*	*184*
Price for youngsters	*17.50*	*18.50*	*16.50*
Suitable for groups	*no*	*no*	*yes*
Suitable for families	*not in the text*	*not in the text*	*yes*

Distance to tube	5 min. walk	2 min. walk	short walk
Parking	yes	yes	no
Internet	not in the text	not in the text	yes
Opening times	365 days 24/7 (round the clock)	365 days / every day	March – November

2 **a** London Central
b Oxford Street
c Oxford Street
d St. Pancras

3

I prefer youth hostelling, because …	I prefer camping, because …
• it's like living in a hotel. • a room is more comfortable than a tent. • you are nearer to a city's attractions and sights. • you can have Internet in your room. • …	• it's cheaper. • you are in the open air. • I don't like cities, I prefer nature. • you can go almost anywhere; there's always a campsite near. • you can sit around a camp fire at night. • …

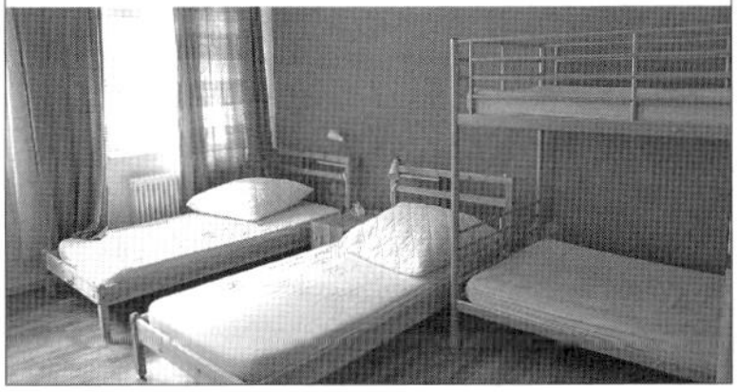

M 4 Cooking Together

1 **a** four
b Minestrone, chicken curry, savoury mince
c cake, muffins
d pizza
e chicken pieces, minced beef, ham, salami

2 pepper, oregano, curry powder, cinnamon, vanilla essence (salt, sugar, vinegar)

3 Individual solutions

4

Meryl	Sandra	Pat	Malcolm	Linda	Alan
Mum's favourite cake	Minestrone	Dad's savoury mince	Sherry trifle	Californian muffins or Mum's favourite cake	Chicken curry

5

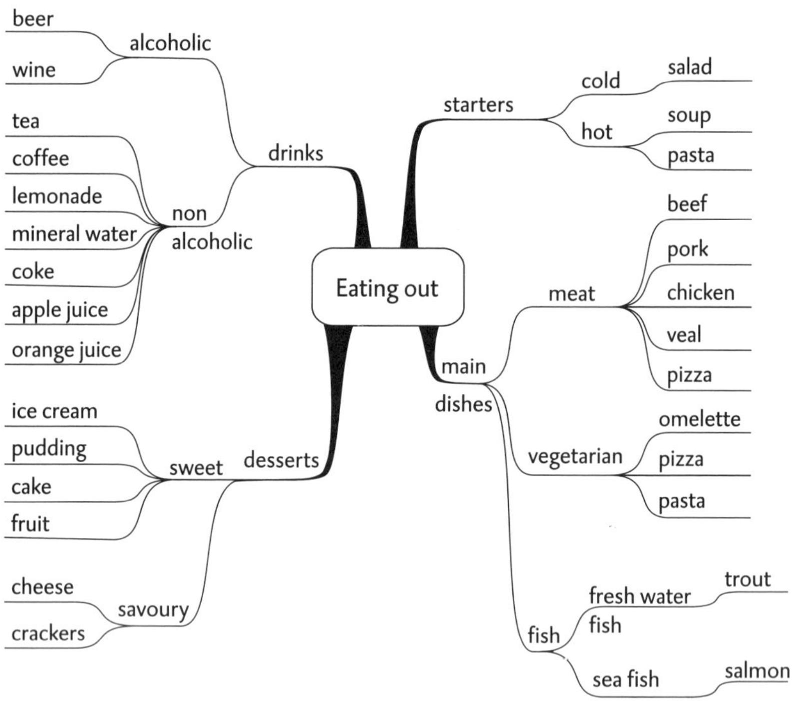

6 Individual solutions

M 5 Road Safety

1 Words that are important to understand the text are marked in this version of the text. You find an explanation for the words in **bold** print below.

The Ministry of Transport will use the latest technology to warn young people of the dangers of **careless** driving. To improve road safety video clips of distracted drivers will be **beamed** directly to youngsters' mobile phones in cinemas **throughout** Scotland using the latest Bluetooth technology. The move was announced by Transport Minister Stewart Stevenson and it comes after research **revealed** that young people are less **likely** to use traditional media like television and are much more likely to respond to mobiles and the Internet. The new technology works by beaming a film clip onto the young person's phone as they arrive in cinema **foyers** and runs together with a new cinema advert from Road Safety Scotland which shows that **momentary distraction** is one of the main causes of road accidents.

Mr Stevenson said: "The latest statistics show a **decrease** in road accidents in Scotland in 2007, but we cannot and will not be satisfied with this development. Too many people are still dying on Scotland's roads and sadly young drivers continue to be **over-represented** in these deaths. "As a **government**, we are constantly looking at new ways to reach this age group and I am **determined** that we look beyond the traditional and towards the innovative in our efforts to save lives. This campaign is new, and it can make a real difference. Ninety seven per cent of young people between 18 and 24 now own a mobile phone. That is a huge audience we can reach with this campaign."

The technology works by beaming an advert onto a young person's phone. Once accepted, the clip showing young people travelling in a car, is interrupted as a text message is **received**. After clicking the message, the clip resumes to show what happens when drivers are distracted. The message 'one distraction is all it takes' then appears.

Difficult words you might have looked up:

- careless: not thinking about what you are doing, so that you make mistakes
- beam: to send a signal through the air
- throughout: in all parts of the country

- (to) reveal: to make something known
- likely: probably *(wahrscheinlich)*
- foyer: a room or hall at the entrance to a public building (e. g. theatre)
- momentary: lasting for a very short time
- distraction: something that stops you paying attention to what you are doing
- decrease: a fall, becoming less
- satisfied: pleased and happy
- over-represented: there are too many young drivers among the people killed in road accidents
- government: the group of people who run a country or state
- (to be) determined: to really want to do something
- (to) receive: (to) get

2 beam: v. *senden*
save: v. *retten*
take: v. *brauchen*

3 **a** The Ministry of Transport will use Bluetooth technology to send videos to the phones of young people.

b This is the best way of reaching young people. This age group doesn't watch TV or doesn't read newspapers but uses mobile phones very often.

c Drivers do not pay attention to the road; perhaps they talk to their friends in the car or they listen to music.

4 ☐ A video message warns teenagers of the dangers of drinking and driving.
☑ A video message tells teenagers to drive carefully.
☐ A video message tells teenagers not to use mobile phones in cinemas.

M 6 Teenagers Today

1 **a** The reporter wants to know ...

- [ ] why teenagers always have to wear hoodies.
- [x] what the teenagers think about the image of young people in the eyes of the general public.
- [ ] what teenagers think about older people.

b The teenagers say that some youngsters behave badly because ...

- [ ] between 16 and 18 they hate everybody.
- [ ] they feel too much under pressure.
- [x] they don't know what to do with themselves.

c One of teenagers says ...

- [ ] he always does what his parents tell him to do.
- [x] he doesn't care what his parents tell him to do.
- [ ] he always does the opposite of what his parents tell him.

d The teenagers say about bullying that ...

- [x] it is something you should stay out of.
- [ ] it doesn't happen often in their school.
- [ ] it is very unpleasant if it happens to someone you know.

2 **a** The teenagers are not interested in politics because they think it has nothing to do with them, especially as they are still too young to vote. In addition they don't really know what politics is all about.

b Graeme gets on well with his parents, but when it comes to personal problems he would rather talk to a friend.

c Acts of violence happen where they live, but, on the whole, they believe that there is much less violence than in London.

d I can imagine that there is less violence in Wales than in London, because London is a much bigger place with many more people. In the smaller towns people probably know each other better and are not so aggressive.

3 Titles (top to bottom): *Billy Elliot – The Musical, Hamlet, Swan Lake, Romeo and Juliet, The Mouse Trap*

A	B	C	D	E
–	3	4	1, 5	2

4 possible arguments: price, availability, personal likes or dislikes of certain genres/topics, etc.

5 The best hostel would be: St. Pancras
Reason: suitable for groups

6 **a** When you come out of Leicester Square tube station cross Cranbourn Street and keep walking along Charing Cross Road until you come to the crossing with Shaftesbury Avenue. Take the first small street after the crossing on your left, which is Moor Street and which will take you straight to Old Compton Street. Turn left and you will see the Prince Edward Theatre on the other side of the road.

b Dialogue:

JAMIE: Excuse me, sir, is there a pub nearby where we could go for a coke or something?

THEATRE ATTENDANT: Yes, there is a pub, not far away. It's called the Golden Lion. It's in Dean Street.

JAMIE: Could you tell us, please, how to get there?

THEATRE ATTENDANT: Of course. On leaving the Prince Edward Theatre turn right and walk along Old Compton Street. Then take the second left, Dean Street, and you will find the pub a bit further down, just past the crossing with Romilly Street.

JAMIE: Thank you. The girls in our group would prefer to go to a café for some tea, coffee or hot chocolate. Where could they go?

THEATRE ATTENDANT: Well, they could drop into Costa's.

JAMIE: Could you tell us how to get there, please?

THEATRE ATTENDANT: The café is nearer than the Golden Lion. It's in Old Compton Street, just like the theatre. When you step out of the theatre, turn right, Costa's is on the other side of the Prince Edward at the crossing of Old Compton and Frith Street.

JAMIE: Thank you very much for your help.

THEATRE ATTENDANT: You're welcome. I'm sure you'll find your way and – enjoy your evening.

This is what the publican says:

On leaving the pub turn left and walk down to Shaftesbury Avenue. Turn left into Shaftesbury Avenue and take the first street on your right. This is Gerrard Place, go straight on down there until you get into Newport Place. At the end of Newport Place turn left again into Little Newport Street which will take you to Charing Cross Road. Turn right and the tube station is further down on the other side of the road.

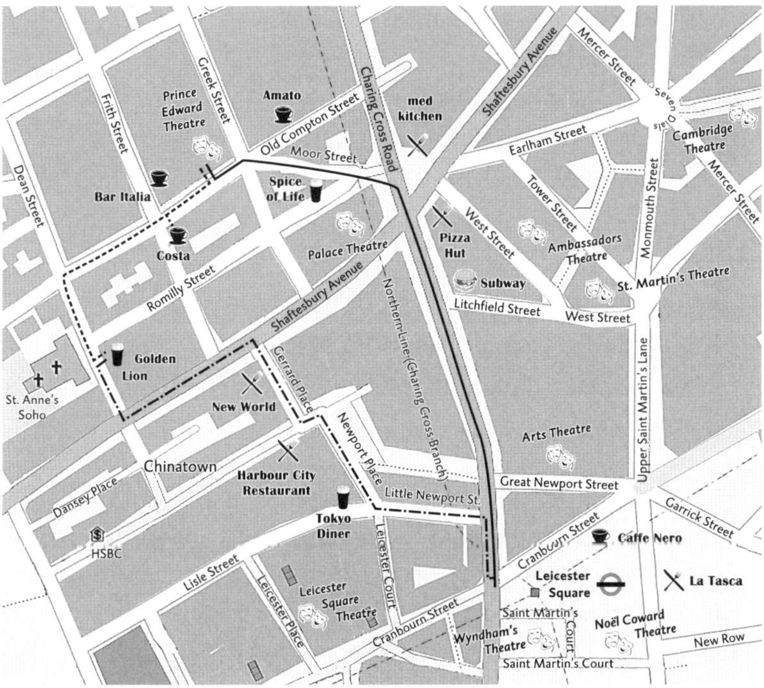

first route second route third route

M7 Do Something Funny for Money

1

	true	false	not in the text
Richard Curtis comes from Africa.	☐	☑	☐
Jane Tewson first had the idea for Comic Relief.	☑	☐	☐
Bob Geldof founded Comic Relief.	☐	☑	☐
Hunger is a big problem in Africa.	☑	☐	☐
Today money from Comic Relief also goes to the UK.	☑	☐	☐
Red Nose Day takes place twice a year.	☐	☑	☐
On Red Nose Day kids do not go to school.	☐	☑	☐
On Red Nose Day people dress up like clowns.	☐	☑	☐
The more traditional events are less successful.	☐	☐	☑
Famous people raised one and a half million pounds by climbing Mount Kilimanjaro.	☑	☐	☐
The BBC plans all activities in the country.	☐	☑	☐
Germany has its own Red Nose Day every two years.	☐	☐	☑

2 **a** "something had to be done" (ll. 6/7)

b "for the fight against hunger" (l. 12)

c "a vicar even illuminated one tower of his church red" (ll. 36/37)

d "to attract attention to the good cause" (l. 37)

3 **a** They started Comic Relief to support people in Africa, especially in Eritrea and Ethiopia, who had nothing to eat and died in great numbers from starvation.

b They concentrated on African countries because these nations were extremely poor and help was needed there most.

c Farmers in Ethiopia and Eritrea could not produce enough food for the population; therefore food had to be imported. Comic Relief gave money to make these imports possible.

d Red Nose Day is a very special day, because on this day the whole nation takes part in collecting money for a good cause.

e I think it's such a success in Britain, because the British have a great sense of humour and they like strange and sometimes weird ideas or eccentric people. The fun is even greater when you can combine your extraordinary behaviour with doing something for others who need your help.

4 Individual solutions

5 I think a lot of money should be spent on improving people's health. In Africa, many parents and their children fall ill, because they do not have enough to eat or because they don't eat the right food. In the hot and dry climate crops do not grow properly and harvests often fail. Most African governments are too poor to buy food on the world market and consequently the population suffers from hunger and malnutrition. Comic Relief money could be used to buy food overseas and distribute it to hungry people. However, this should only be done for a short time. For a long-time solution of the food problem the organisation should invest money in the improvement of farming methods to help farmers increase the agricultural output. In addition, medical services should be made available, especially for Africans who live in rural areas. The money could be spent on training doctors to make regular visits and on the building of hospitals. Another important reason why people are often ill is the lack of hygiene. Many poor people live in shacks where they do not have access to fresh clean water. All in all, the money collected by Comic Relief should be spent to enable people to live in decent conditions, and, most important of all, on teaching them to help themselves. *(221 words)*

M8 Going West – Part 1

1

	true	false	not in the text
Paddy left Ireland because he wanted to find gold in the New World.	☐	☑	☐
Paddy and his brother Frank left Ireland together and set up a farm in Kentucky.	☐	☑	☐
Adam O'Hearne wanted to become an engineer.	☐	☐	☑

After Amy was born Molly agreed to go West.	✓		
The wagon train started from Kentucky.		✓	

2 **a** "rather small and quiet town" (l. 22)

b "with the financial help from Molly's brother Frank and Adam's employer, Mr Wilson, Paddy was able to buy ..." (ll. 29/30)

c "Captain Shadrack, who informed all emigrants to provide themselves above all with flour, bacon, coffee, sugar and salt." (ll. 33/34)

3 First paragraph: Leaving home
Second paragraph: An adventurous plan
Third paragraph: Preparing for the trek
Fourth paragraph: An easy start

4

A	They travelled until sunset, when they set up camp for the night.	4
B	Because of the heavy snowfall they could hardly see where they were going.	–
C	But Molly didn't want to go on a journey which would last for months – especially as she was pregnant again.	2
D	Shortly after their arrival their third child, Laura, was born.	1
E	The journey to the Far West could only be made during the summer months and before the first snowfall.	3

5 **a** Paddy O'Hearne worked on the farm of his brother-in-law together with his younger son Luke. Adam, Luke's elder brother, found a job in a hardware store in town.

b Somebody had told him that gold had been found in California. He wanted to join the gold diggers.

c The pioneers, who used oxen to pull their wagons, had to wait until the winter was over so that the cattle could feed on the fresh grass.

d The first part of the journey was not difficult for the pioneers because there were no rivers or mountains to cross and people, and cattle had enough to eat and drink.

M 9 Going West – Part 2

1 First paragraph: The difficulties begin
Second paragraph: Illnesses, deaths and a rebellion
Third paragraph: Arrival in the land of dreams

2

A	B	C	D	E	F
5	3	6	1	2	4

3

a When the boys could not find any **wood**, the people used **buffalo dung** to make a fire.

b Before the settlers could **cross** a river, they had to **unload** their wagons.

c On later treks, the whites **killed (off)** too many buffalo, so that the Indians began to **attack** the pioneers.

d Mr Judd and his group **left** the trek, because they wanted to carry on **faster/on their own**.

4

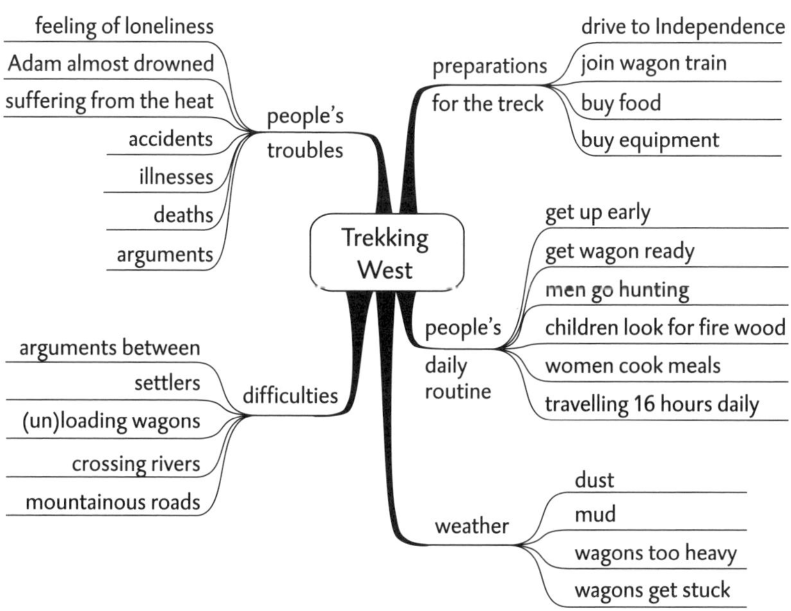

5

Questions	Your partner's answers
Why did you support your father's wish to move west?	We just thought it would be exciting to experience something new. We knew what work on a farm or in a shop was like and found it boring at times. So we were looking forward very much to going to a place where nobody had been before and making a new start. It seemed a great adventure and a great possibility.
Were you not frightened about having to start a new life in the wilds, all on your own?	Oh, no, on the contrary. We knew our father could work hard – and our mother as well. And we were keen on supporting our dad. We wanted to learn new things like building a block house for example or go hunting and fishing.
What, in your opinion, was the most difficult bit during the long trek?	To be honest, I'd say it was boredom. No, really. Of course there were the Indians, there were illnesses, hunger, rain and so on. But, on the whole, we found it very often boring – moving on and on and on. The journey seemed endless, and at times we thought, we would never make it.
Weren't you scared of the Indians?	Yes, at first we were. We had never seen any real Indians before. But, I believe, they were just as frightened of us as we were of them. We made friends with one young Indian. His name was Yellow Fish and he and his father helped us a lot. They even saved Adam's life. We were quite sad when they left us.

M10 The Lord from the Poor Side of Town

1 First paragraph: An early start after school
Second paragraph: Selling and earning millions
Third paragraph: Years of frustration
Fourth paragraph: Rising to star fame
Fifth paragraph: In the firing line

2 **a** "Alan, (...), left school without any qualifications" (ll. 4/5)

b "He did not like his work; he wanted to be self-employed" (ll. 6/7)

c "a combination of the first letters of his name and the word 'trading'" (ll. 11/12)

d "a special talent for sensing new developments" (l. 14)

e "but trouble came in the 1990s" (ll. 18/19) / "eventually the company lost many customers" (ll. 20/21) / "the failure" (l. 21)

3 **a** Alan Sugar was disappointed because …

- ☐ Jürgen Klinsmann did not play well.
- ☐ he did not like the German player.
- ☑ Klinsmann did not want to stay in England.
- ☐ Klinsmann wanted more money.

b After his time with Tottenham, Alan Sugar …

- ☐ was so disappointed that he retired from all his businesses.
- ☑ began to work in television.
- ☐ began to buy property in London.
- ☐ counted his profits from the club management.

c *The Apprentice* …

- ☐ is a new game show.
- ☐ is a programme in which TV viewers choose the winner.
- ☐ tests if candidates are good singers.
- ☑ offers candidates a chance to start work for Alan Sugar.

d Some people criticize Alan Sugar because …

- ☑ he is so aggressive.
- ☐ he sets difficult tasks.
- ☐ he is the only person to decide on the winner.
- ☐ his tasks have nothing to do with real life.

4 Possible arguments:

Yes, this is a good show, because …	No, this is not a good show, because …
• it's fun to watch. • it's exciting. • people can show what they are good at. • it gives the viewers an idea about the business world.	• it's all about making money. • it gives viewers the impression that you have to be hard and egoistic. • it makes candidates look like idiots. • it seems an expensive programme and therefore a waste of money.

5 a

	true	false	not in the text
Reality TV shows are mainly an American invention.	✓		
TV stations in other countries adapt the American version.	✓		
The show *Big Brother* was developed in the Netherlands.			✓
Viewers can phone in, but the TV bosses decide on the winner.			✓
Paul Potts and Susanne Boyle won first prizes in *The Apprentice*.		✓	

b
- When a show is popular in the United States, **other countries produce their national version**.
- When *Big Brother* was first shown on TV, **it was heavily criticised**.
- The term "reality show" is wrong, because **these programmes have nothing to do with reality**.
- The TV companies want many viewers to phone in, because **they earn a lot of money from the telephone calls**.

c

Yes, I would take part, because …	No, I wouldn't take part, because …
• I've always wanted to be on TV. • I like challenges. • I might find a job that way. • I think it's just fun. • I want to become famous. • I want to make money. • …	• I'm too nervous. • I don't want to make a fool of myself in front of millions of viewers. • I don't like showing off with what I can do. • I hate the business world and all that money making. • I'd rather keep a low profile. • …

6 a

VOLUNTARY WORK PLACEMENTS

You may have already done some work *experience*, but doing a further placement while you are at school can be *useful* in your career planning.

Why do a voluntary work placement?

Work placements give you …

- a chance to find out more about a *career* you are considering.
- some practical experience and talking to people who already do the job.
- a better idea of whether it would *suit* you.
- a better chance of standing out when *applying* for courses and jobs.

How long do work placements last?

- Many work placements involve working full-time for a fixed *time* usually six to twelve weeks – but they're often timed to fit in with school *holidays*.

How to find a work placement

- Check national newspapers, especially the *Saturday* editions.
  Many organisations advertise placements at different times of the year.
- Look up the *websites* of firms.
- If you're currently at school, ask the careers office whether they can help you find a placement.
- You may also contact organisations directly, even if they are not advertising.

Remember: A work placement generally does not *earn* you much money – more than once you do not earn anything at all. But work experience can be more valuable than *cash*.

b

Jeff	Chris	Emily	Seth	Sarah	Lily
B	A	C	E	D	A

Lösungsheft zu:
Arbeitsheft Englisch Bildungsstandards Mittlerer Schulabschluss – *Reading*
Best.-Nr. 101550

3 Which text passage tells you that …

a Shantell Steve grew up without the love of caring parents?

____

____

b Jasmin, Adoni and Shantell didn't need anybody to tell them what to do in life?

____

____

c the media give you the impression that success comes easy?

____

____

d it is possible that you have to do work at school which you don't like?

____

____

4 Put the sentences in the correct order as they come up in the text.

A He has had a severe illness ever since he was born.
B He became a professional basketball player even though he was once excluded from his school basketball team.
C With her program she helps young people who are in a difficult situation.
D She will be the first in her family to have a doctor's degree.
E It wasn't easy for her to find a publisher for her first novel.

1	2	3	4	5

5 Match these sentence halves.

A If you don't succeed the first time you try, …
B In order to get good marks at school …
C Sometimes you won't like what you have to do, because …
D It is not so important what you do, but …
E If dreams don't come true, …

1 … you have to do it properly.
2 … you mustn't be disappointed.
3 … you have to work hard.
4 … you don't know yet what it is good for.
5 … you have to try again.

A	B	C	D	E

6 Answer these questions on the text, using your own words.

a What is President Obama's main message to students?

b Why does the President mention the examples of J.K. Rowling and Michael Jordan?

c In which way can you profit from a failure?

d What does he say about troublemakers?